THE wild weather book

book

loads of things to
do outdoors in rain,
wind and snow

fiona danks and jo schofield

For Connie, Dan, Edward, Hannah and Jake

Frances Lincoln Ltd
4 Torriano Mews
Torriano Avenue
London NW5 2RZ
www.franceslincoln.com
www.goingwild.net

The Wild Weather Book

First Frances Lincoln edition: 2013

A catalogue record for this book is available from the
British Library.

ISBN 978-0-7112-3255-6

Printed and bound in China

contents

rain doesn't stop play

Imagine jumping in the biggest puddle you can find, or playing barefoot and feeling squidgy mud ooze up between your toes. How about letting the wind push you along or building your own igloo in the snow? There's no need to stay cooped up when it's wet, windy or cold. Wild weather's a great opportunity to get wrapped up in warm clothes and waterproofs and rush outside for some fun.

Give your bath toys an outdoor adventure; make streamers and go wind dancing, with the streamers whirling around you; make snow mazes or ice toffee; create a glistening ice castle: these are just a few of the exciting, funny and creative adventures you can get up to in the natural world on bad weather days. So don't wait for the sunshine: put this book in your pocket and run outside for a wild weather adventure. The trick to enjoying playing/ being outside in bad weather is to be fully prepared, with:

The right clothes keep warm and dry with:
● Waterproof jacket and trousers, or an all-in-one waterproof suit. Always wear the bottoms of your waterproof trousers outside your boots so that water doesn't drip down on to your socks. Choose a rain jacket with a hood.
● Several layers of clothes rather than one thick layer: if you get too warm you can just remove a layer. Keep your neck warm with a polo neck and a scarf.
● Old clothes: remember that it's fine to get dirty and have fun!
● Wellies or sturdy boots, and long warm socks that make your toes feel cosy and don't slip down inside your wellies. Two pairs of socks are better than one.
● A good hat: one that's warm and weatherproof, and won't blow off in the wind.
● Waterproof gloves: essential to enjoy playing with snow and ice. Take along a few extra pairs, just in case.

Bad weather adventure bag pack a waterproof kit bag with some or all of the following:
● First aid kit (and make sure someone knows how to use it).
● A shelter-making kit: perhaps a simple pop-up tent, a tarpaulin or a big plastic sheet, and some string or cord.
● Plastic bags, to sit on.
● Torch, to extend short winter days. A head torch is best; choose one with

a red light, as this is less disruptive to wildlife.

● Toys: plastic animals, bucket and spade, and anything else that might be fun to play with outdoors.

● Fire-lighting kit (see page 19).

● Camera or mobile phone.

● Umbrellas and some spare clothes.

● Drinks and snacks: essential, in case anyone gets a bit cold or needs an energy boost. Choose things that need little preparation and won't make a mess.

● Flasks of warm drinks (hot chocolate, warm squash or soup). Or, better still, take a Kelly kettle and a few dry sticks so that you can make a hot drink wherever you are.

● A bottle of drinking water.

Once you've had some fun out in the elements, when the weather has hurled its worst at you, go back indoors and get warm and dry as soon as you can. You'll feel a wonderful tingly glow in your fingers and toes. Tuck into a hot chocolate (or other warm drink) and a nourishing snack, and you'll find they've never tasted so good!

With all the projects in this book, follow the safety guidelines on pages 124–5. Some activities are easy to try and others are more challenging; remember that what is easy for one person may be tricky for another. The activity code below provides some guidance as to levels of difficulty and risk, but always take care when playing outdoors.

◊ May be possible to do on your own

◊◊ Some tricky bits which might need a little adult help

◊◊◊ Adult supervision essential

1

rainy days

01

go on a rainy day expedition and picnic

Don't let wet weather put you off: just get wrapped up, pack up a tasty picnic and head outdoors for an adventure. With boots, waterproofs, a hat, gloves and an umbrella you will be ready for anything, so get outside and discover the rainy day secrets of your favourite wild places. Find somewhere to sit under the cover of trees or make your own simple tarpaulin shelter where you can enjoy your picnic while listening to the rain falling all around you.

rainbow hunting

Can anyone find treasure at the end of the rainbow? Hunt for rainbows on a rainy day when the sun is shining from behind you.

Make your own rainbows Take a collecting bag and go in search of natural materials in rainbow colours. How many can you find? Collect little pieces of each colour and stick them onto bits of cardboard covered in double-sided tape.

If you can't remember the colours of the rainbow and their order, use the first letters of each word in this sentence to remind you: Richard Of York Gave Battle In Vain – red, orange, yellow, green, blue, indigo, violet.

03

make a tarpaulin shelter

With some cord and a good tarpaulin (available from outdoor shops and army surplus suppliers) you can make a shelter wherever you are and whatever the weather. If you don't have any tent pegs, use stones or sticks instead. If you don't have a tarp, take along a simple lightweight or pop-up tent, or a large sheet of plastic.

In the woods Find two trees about 2.5m/8ft apart with bare ground in between. Secure the end of a length of cord around one tree and then take it around the other tree and secure tightly

with a knot, making a ridge for the shelter. Hang the tarp over the ridge. Tie guy ropes to each corner and peg them to the ground.

In an open area Take along a couple of tent poles, or find some long sticks, and use them to construct your makeshift shelter.

At the beach Try making a shelter right next to some rocks, and search for some driftwood to support the front of the tarp.

In very wet or cold conditions Use cord to make a low line between two trees or posts. Hang a quarter of the tarp over one side of the cord and the rest on the other side, so that you have enough fabric to fold over the ground to make a groundsheet to protect you from the cold or wet.

make an emergency natural shelter

Do you think it's possible to make a waterproof natural shelter with just sticks and leaves? Well, it definitely is, and here's how:

● Go to some woodland with plenty of fallen sticks and leaf litter. Choose a good spot for a shelter, such as beside a large fallen log or a tree with a low branch.

● Collect lots of long straight dead sticks and lean them against the branch or log. Make sure the sticks are as close together as you can get them.

● Thatch the shelter with leaf litter collected from the woodland floor. First place handfuls of leaf litter against the sticks at ground level and then work right up to the top. The thatch should be at least 30cm/12in thick; if you can see through it, the rain will definitely find a way through.

Spray the shelter with a water pistol to test if it is waterproof. You could make your shelter on a dry day and then try it out on a wet day to see if it keeps you dry.

05

make a natural umbrella

If you are caught out in a rainstorm without wet weather gear, go in search of some big leaves and make a natural umbrella or a funny hat to shelter under.

Leaf umbrella Search for the biggest leaf you can find. Pick it with a long stalk so that you can hold it over your head.

Leaf hat Lay leaves in layers over each other, with the stalks all in the middle, and tie together with raffia. Make sure some of the raffia is long enough to tie round your chin.

For a more stylish leaf hat, take one large leaf and wrap it round to make a sort of Robin Hood hat. Pin in place, using grass stems or a feather, and decorate with a range of natural materials woven through the leaf. (See pages 5 and 9.)

make an umbrella den

Find as many brightly coloured umbrellas as you can. Arrange them to make a fun multi-coloured den to shelter in with your friends. Or huddle under a big clear dome-shaped umbrella so that you can stay dry while looking out at the rainy world.

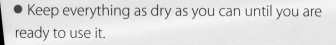

making fire in the rain

Knowing how to light fire in the rain could make all the difference to your survival, or at least provide some warmth and comfort. Are you up for the challenge? Before starting, read the fire safety tips on page 125.

- Keep everything as dry as you can until you are ready to use it.

- Choose a spot out of the wind and the worst of the rain, but not near overhanging trees or over tree roots. This fire was made in a cave entrance.

- Search for the driest wood, which snaps on breaking. Look under trees or bushes, or collect dead sticks that haven't yet fallen to the ground. Stack the wood near your fire place so that it will dry out once the fire is alight.

- If the ground is very wet and you don't have a fire pan, break some straight sticks into 60cm/2ft lengths. Lay them side by side to make a square base for your fire.

- Use plenty of tinder and kindling to get the fire going quickly.

What to take with you

● A spark-making fire steel.

● Dry tinder (e.g. dried leaves or grass, fluffy seeds or toilet paper) in a waterproof container.

● Feather sticks. Use a sharp knife to cut thin curls along a stick until you have a series of thin feathers (as illustrated) that will catch alight easily.

● A fire pan (this could be an old wok or wheel hub), so that you can light your fire off the damp ground.

08

rain shadows

Try this out with some friends during a short sharp summer rainstorm. When you see rain approaching, lie down on a hard surface – perhaps a patio or school playground – before it gets too wet. Look up at the sky and feel the cool rain falling on you. Once the storm has passed, jump up and have a look at your rain shadow.

● Try making rain shadows at the beach, on a rock or on a pavement. Where else can you make them?

● Try making groups of rain shadows. How many friends can you persuade to join you? What shapes can you make?

● If it's not raining, make your own rain with a hose or a water spray bottle, and try making rain shadows of hands or feet in patterns.

● If you want to be really prepared, keep a suitable space covered with a groundsheet or a large piece of plastic, so that when it rains you will be sure of having a dry area on which to make a rain shadow.

09

rain painting

Let a shower of rain transform simple pictures into multicoloured masterpieces.

● Draw pictures on plain white kitchen paper, using brightly coloured water-soluble pens.

● Hang the pictures on a washing line and let the rain mix the colours. Experiment with different papers, inks and paints.

● Try drawing patterns of dots and lines. What does the rain do to them? Let the pictures dry and then press them flat if need be.

rain stencils

These rain shadows of natural materials won't last long, so have a camera ready to take a picture before they disappear. You'll need to prepare before it starts raining.

● Collect leaves of different shapes and sizes. Find a space on a patio or some paving, or put some sand in a tray and level the surface.

● Arrange leaves or other natural materials into a pattern or a picture in your chosen space. If it's windy, put stones on the leaves so that they won't blow away.

● Wait for a rain shower. Once it stops, pick up the leaves to reveal your stencil patterns. See if people can guess what natural materials you used by looking at the patterns.

rain music and drums

Rain spatters against a windowpane, plops on to trees and drips off leaves. It thunders on to metal or plastic and falls softly into puddles. Such sounds have inspired music and song lyrics, lulled people to sleep and even been used to measure the size of raindrops.

Recording the rain Go outside on a rainy day and use a mobile phone or iPod to record the sounds of rain in different places. Replay your recording when you are warm and snug in your bed. Will it lull you to sleep, perhaps?

Make rain music Raid the recycling bin and the kitchen cupboards for things that might make a noise when rain falls on them. How about cooking tins, old food tins, a metal dustbin lid, or plastic boxes, some covered with silver foil? Experiment with different materials.

   Place your collection of containers outdoors in a rainstorm, or perhaps under a leaking drainpipe or an upturned umbrella with a hole in it. What different sounds do they make?

dancing and singing in the rain

If you've been cooped up indoors on a wet day, why not get your waterproofs on and enjoy some singing and dancing in the rain? Or, if the weather is warm, forget the waterproofs!

● Sing a favourite song while dancing in the rain, or a song with a rainy theme. Try 'Singin' in the Rain', 'Incy Wincy Spider', 'Rain, rain, go away and come again another day'.

● Make laminated song sheets of your favourite rainy day songs, all ready to take out into the wet.

● Invent some silly songs to sing while walking along in a rainstorm, or to remind you later of being out in a favourite place in the rain.

Make simple home-made musical instruments to accompany your songs – sticks with bells on, simple maracas (jam jars full of seeds) or rattles (sticks with ring pulls).

13

go on a puddle hunt

Pull on your wellies and go on a puddle hunt. Who can find the biggest puddles or the muddiest puddles? Or try some of these puddle games:

● Can you jump over puddles? Have a long jump competition.

● Jump in puddles and see who can make the biggest splash. Remember: only splash other people if you don't mind being splashed in return!

● Try a puddle obstacle course, in which you jump from puddle to puddle. Anyone stepping outside the puddles is out of the game.

● Make a stone or stick tower in a puddle. Can you knock it down by throwing stones at it? If you are throwing stones, make sure no one is near by.

● Build a stone castle in the middle of a puddle and make boats and mud people to protect it.

● Where does the rain go? Become a water detective and follow some surface water and find out where it goes. Put a leaf or a stick in the water: will it find its way to a large puddle or a stream, or will it disappear down a drain?

14

cooling off and swimming in the rain

On a hot humid summer's day when a storm is brewing, why not run around outside when the rain starts to fall and enjoy a refreshing open-air shower – such a relief from the heat and humidity. Or after some muddy play, have a wash in nature's power shower!

And how about going for a rainy day swim? Whether in the sea, a river or a lake, swimming in the rain can be really special. Take along a warm drink and put up a tarp shelter so that you have somewhere to get warm and dry quickly after you get out of the water. Wet suits are great for warmth and buoyancy.

Safety tips Only go wild swimming when accompanied by adults and always choose safe, clean shallow waters where swimming is permitted. When swimming in the sea, watch out for currents. Always swim with other people and stay close to the shore. Don't swim in drinking water reservoirs.

tasting raindrops

What flavour are raindrops? Catch them on your tongue and see. Do they taste better in the morning for breakfast or in the evening for tea? Are they sweeter on a warm day or a chilly day? Does summer rain have a hint of strawberry?

16 make a mud slide

Great fun if you don't mind getting plastered in mud!

If it's too muddy and slippery in the rain or snow to stay on your feet, just sit down and slide down a hill instead! Best to wear tough old clothes, and take along a heavy-duty plastic sack to give a little protection to your bottom and make the mud slide even faster.

Tip Only do this on slopes where you won't damage delicate grassland habitats.

make a rain catcher

A simple way to measure the rain.

● Carefully cut the top off a large clear plastic bottle, just below where the bottle starts to taper. Then put the top upside down into what remains of the bottle, so that it's like a funnel.

● Put an elastic band round the middle of the bottle. Poke a ruler down through the elastic band until it is flush with the bottle's base and use this to help you draw a scale on the bottle with a permanent marker, up to about 10cm/4in.

● Remove the ruler and replace it with a thin stick. Place the rain catcher in an open space, pushing the stick into the ground to ensure it doesn't blow away or fall over. If your rain catcher is on a hard surface, put pebbles in the bottom to make it stable.

● How clean is the rain? Place a small sieve lined with kitchen roll in the top of the rain catcher. Is any dirt left behind on the paper?

Measure how much rain falls each day. Can you collect enough to drink? Does your rainwater taste different from tap water?

after the rain

18

make a water run

This fun challenge is a bit like making a marble run. Can you keep water flowing along an obstacle course without losing any on the way?

● You will need a collection of empty plastic bottles and containers, funnels and pouring cups, metal cans (beware of sharp edges) or even some old plastic guttering or water pipes – anything that can be made into a channel for water to flow down.

● Find some muddy puddles and push a few forked sticks into the mud. Cut bottles in half lengthways to make channels and fix them together by pushing them into cans. Make channels at different heights, checking that water can flow from one to the other.

● Pour puddle water down your run to see how well it works. If it starts to rain heavily, see if the rainwater rushes down your run.

● How far can you get the water to flow? Can you race little sticks or other natural materials down the run?

● Have a water run competition. Each team makes their own water run and puts a large container at the bottom to collect the water. The winning team is the one that collects the most water in the shortest time.

Outdoor adventures for the bath toys

Why should the bath toys always stay indoors? Just imagine all the adventures they could have out in the big wide world, especially after a rainstorm.

● Rain is perfect weather for ducks. Let the toy ducks have a race in a stream or across a muddy puddle.

● Take the bath boats for a ride, pulling them along behind you.

● Take the pouring toys outside and have fun playing pouring games with muddy puddle water.

● Make sure you wash the toys before you use them in the bath again.

Let the toy ducks have a race in a stream or across a muddy puddle on a rainy day.

41

Water droplet scavenger hunt

Have you ever watched raindrops slither and slide down a windowpane? Once the rain has stopped, go and hunt for droplets of rain outside on leaves, seed heads, twigs, spiders' webs and anywhere else they might gather.

● Who can find water droplets in the most different places?

● Can you photograph them and build up a gallery of water droplet pictures?

● Can you see reflections in them? Or how about using a magnifying glass to investigate them more closely?

● Try collecting a few droplets in a little container. Perhaps they could be the key ingredient for a magic potion or a wicked spell!

21

make a noah's ark

Poor old Noah: how did he ever collect all those animals and live on the ark with them? Have a go at making your own little ark to play with when the rain stops.

● First make your ark. This one was made from polystyrene with cardboard stuck around it to make the boat shape and the cabin, but any old plastic bottles or juice cartons would do. Or make one out of sticks and old plastic bottles tied together with string, which won't get so soggy when wet.

● Use clay and natural materials such as twigs, bark, leaves and wool to make as many different animals as you can. Be sure to make them in pairs so that the animals can go into the ark two by two. Use your imagination: a nutshell makes a great tortoise, twigs can become legs or antlers, and leaves can become rabbits' ears or squirrels' tails.

Take your ark full of animals outside and see if it floats on a puddle.

floating and sinking

● Go for a walk after rain and collect natural materials such as bark, sticks, shells, feathers, seeds and nuts. See if you can guess which things will float and which will sink.

● Place your collection of natural materials in a big puddle to see if they float or sink. Did you guess correctly? Try making little boats out of all the things that float.

messing about with boats

- How about taking a whole fleet of toy boats outside to race across puddles or play in rainy day streams? Perhaps your boats will explore new territories or have a battle with an enemy fleet.

- Create imaginary worlds and characters, like this mud-and-stick man taking his boat into the safety of a harbour.

- Try making boats out of natural materials such as sticks, rushes or bark, or add a few recycled materials such as corks and plastic. Add a weight or keel to help keep the boats upright, and then test how well they float. Tie a large glossy leaf on to a length of string and pull it through puddles with a stick man passenger aboard.

soggy worlds

After a rainstorm, head outside with a ball of clay and lots of imagination. Can you make up your own soggy worlds with clay creatures, such as this Loch Ness monster on her nest preying on the little clay ducks?

make a mud pit in the garden

Make a mud pit, perhaps in a corner of the garden, and have fun being a mud lark. How muddy can you get? Wear your oldest clothes and if anyone fusses about the dirt just tell them that good clean mud comes out in the wash!

● Get out the beach toys or some small garden tools and have a go at building houses for mud people or caves for mud monsters.

● Try making imaginary worlds with mountains and volcanoes, lakes and rivers, roads and railways. Take the toy cars or the toy soldiers or animals out for an exciting adventure in your magical muddy world.

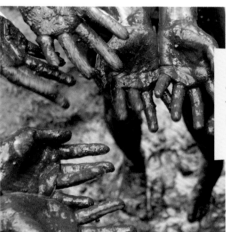

Let gloopy mud dribble through your fingers and squelch up between your toes.

dam a puddle or a rainy day stream

Go on an expedition after rain to look for a line of puddles or a temporary stream. Can you make dams with mud, sticks and stones? Make little pools, and then release the water into another puddle or back into the stream; or try to fill one huge puddle. How far can you float a leaf or a feather down your stream?

make mud pies

Take some old pots and pans outside and make a mud-pie kitchen in the mud pit. Have fun mixing, moulding and making pies, cakes and other wonderful concoctions. Happy cooking!

● Mix mud with sand, sawdust and crushed leaves to add different colours and textures.

● How about making mud cakes to celebrate the birthdays of your friends, your toys or the fairies in the woods? Decorate them with twig candles, and add some moss or coloured leaves as icing and perhaps pebbles and shells as sweets on top, or add a few fresh herbs for their scent.

28

mud sculptures

Wet sticky mud is perfect for moulding and sculpting.

Mud balls Roll mud into different-sized balls. Cover each ball in natural materials – perhaps moss, grass, sticks, leaves or petals – and then place the mud balls on top of each other. How high can you make your mud-ball tower? Alternatively, make covered mud balls round a stick or a branch.

Mud decorations Make a mud ball around a short stick with some string tied on to it. Decorate the ball with natural materials. Hang it from a tree or take it indoors to hang in a window.

Tree monsters Can you bring a twisted old tree to life with a scary or funny mud face?

Pinch pots Roll some clayey mud into a ball about the size of a tennis ball. Insert your thumb to make a well. Pinch up the walls of the pot while turning it slowly in your hands to ensure an even thickness all the way round. Pat the base on to a smooth surface to make it flat. Wet your hands and smooth the pot's surface before letting it dry.

29 mud castles

Just as you go to the beach to make sandcastles, why not go outdoors near where you live, find a mud patch and have a wonderful messy time making mud castles?

Mould sticky mud into crazy imaginary fortresses and palaces, using stones and sticks for the structure and other natural materials to add details such as windows or flags. Add tunnels, secret rooms, dark dungeons and deep moats, and make little mud and stick knights to defend the castle against intruders.

puddle reflections

On a calm windless day discover the world reflected in puddles. Can you see yourself, your friends, the sky or the trees? Take photos of the best reflections you can find, or try making some wild reflections.

● Float natural objects on puddles to make reflections. How about making reflection puppets using natural materials in your hand, like this funny snappy monster?

mud painting

Use a stick to draw in a mud patch, or mix mud with water to make a natural paint. For a smooth paint, strain the mud mixture through an old sieve. If you want to make other colours, add mashed-up chalk or berries or some crushed charcoal.

Mud pictures Paint mud pictures on card, thick paper or old slates, or draw mud graffiti on an outside wall or the patio (only do this somewhere where it's easy to wash the mud off – best to check with a grown-up first). Or for some nature graffiti, paint mud on a tree trunk or a rock.

Mud stencils Place a leaf on a log, a slate, a paving stone or some paper. Paint mud over and around the leaf. Lift the leaf to reveal a stencil.

Leaf patterns Cover a tough evergreen leaf with a layer of mud paint. Using a feather quill, scratch patterns in the mud.

Make henna-style body paint Cover your arms or legs in clean mud (it feels nice and is good for the skin!). Use a feather quill to scrape swirling patterns or draw pictures of animals or flowers in the mud.

chalk painting

Coloured chalks are fun to use outdoors after the rain, spreading easily and smoothly over a wet surface. This chalk butterfly was drawn on wet paving stones; what plants or animals can you draw outside after the rain?

33

play stuck in the mud

You may have played Stuck in the Mud tag where whoever is tagged has to stand with his or her legs apart until another player crawls between their legs to release them. But have you ever played Stuck in the Mud for real?

● Search for the stickiest mud you can find, perhaps in a muddy track or field, and have some fun getting stuck.

● Or play real Stuck in the Mud: if you are tagged, go and jump in the mud and stay there until your friends release you.

Safety tip Never play in deep mud. Play only in mud where you know there is solid ground not far below the surface, such as along a track or bridleway.

play barefoot

After a warm summer rainstorm, go exploring without shoes. Feel wet grasses tickle your feet or squidgy mud ooze up between your toes; or try some puddle paddling. Here are some other fun barefoot things to do.

Hand and foot prints Make wet muddy foot and hand prints on rolls of lining paper, on pavements or patios, or even on your friends!

Hand and foot casts Find some squidgy mud and make hand and foot prints. Place a circle of card around a print, as shown. Make a creamy mixture of plaster of Paris and pour into the circle of card so that the print is completely covered. Leave the plaster to set for about twenty minutes. Carefully pick up the cast and scrape off the mud to reveal a permanent memento of your hand or foot.

Blindfold barefoot trail Lay a rope trail through the garden or at the park. Check there are no sharp bits and pieces on the ground and then try following the trail blindfolded and barefoot.

35

the great snail hunt

After a rainstorm go out with a torch just as it's getting dark. How many snails can you find slithering around your garden or at the park?

Make a snailery Find a large glass or clear plastic container – perhaps an old sweetie jar or even a fish tank. Put damp soil, leaves, bits of wood and stones in the bottom with a little water and some fresh green leaves. Collect some snails and put them in your snailery, and then keep an eye on what they eat and how they behave. Only keep the snails for a short while before returning them to where you found them.

The great snail swap Collect a few snails and paint a spot of nail varnish on their shells. Let them go somewhere in the garden, or swap snails with a friend who lives near by. A few days later, go outside after rain and see how many marked snails you can find.

A version of this was run as an official experiment to see how far snails wander; for further information, go to www.bbc.co.uk and search for the Great Snail Swap.

go on an animal hunt

Some animals love warm wet conditions, so after a summer rainstorm go outside and have a good look around to see what wildlife you can spot. Take a magnifying glass and look for little creatures as well as bigger creatures.

● Birds know that after a rainstorm is the best time to look for worms, which wriggle up to the surface of the soil. It's also worth looking out for slugs, snails, slowworms (legless lizards), frogs, newts and hedgehogs.

● Set up a Worm Rescue Squad with your friends: your mission is to go and rescue worms stranded on pavements or patios after the rain. Gently put them in a bucket of mud and return them to a grassy area or a flower bed.

Safety tip Always wash hands after handling slugs and snails.

make a wormery

The best way to see why worms are the gardener's best friend is to make a wormery.

● Go out after rain and collect a few worms in a bucket of damp soil. Find a large glass jar with a lid or cut the top off a big plastic bottle. Add alternate layers of sand, moist soil and dead leaves. Leave a 5cm/2in space at the top.

● Put the worms in the wormery and add some dead leaves, grass and a few vegetable or fruit peelings (perhaps from the compost bin). Replace the lid of the jar or the top of the bottle, and pierce a few holes in it so that the worms have a supply of fresh air.

● Worms hate light, so cover the wormery with dark fabric or paper and put it somewhere cool for about a week.

After a week or so, look at the wormery and see what the worms have done. Can you see where they have been burrowing? What has happened to the leaves? Release the worms back into the garden.

make a track trap

Have you ever wondered what wild creatures visit your garden, or the local countryside or park, at night?

● Find a muddy patch along a track or in the garden – somewhere you think might be used by animals. Using a stick, scrape a smooth area of mud. Place some sticks around the area to mark exactly where your track trap is. If you wish, put a little pet food in the middle of the track trap.

● Leave the trap overnight and then go back in the morning to see if there are any telltale tracks in the mud. Can you work out who has visited?

● For a portable track trap, find an old tray and cover it in a smooth layer of soft squidgy mud. Place it outside overnight with a tempting snack in the middle and see if you can work out who has come to call! For how to make plaster casts of the tracks, see page 59.

3

windy days

39 feeling the wild wind

The wind is a mysterious, wild force that we can't see but we can feel. On a wild windy day rush outside and find a big open space, or run to the top of a high hill. Can you feel the wind's strength? Is it fierce or friendly? Lean into the wind: is it strong enough to support you? Open your coat and let the wind blow it around you like a sail – but watch out, you may take off! Let the wind steal your screams as it gusts and blows all around you.

40

blowing bubbles in the wind

Chasing bubbles on a windy day is a great way to keep warm and have fun! How many bubbles can you catch? How far will they go? Where will the wind carry them?

DIY bubbles This home-made bubble potion can work better than bought bubble mixtures. Mix together: 1 part washing-up liquid (you might need to experiment with different types, as not all washing-up liquids make good bubbles), 8 parts water, 1 part glycerine.

Can you use bubbles to find out which way the wind is blowing?

41

make wind flags and flying creatures

Enjoy playing in the wind with homemade flying creatures and wind flags. You can also use the flags in games like Capture the Flag.

Flying creatures

● Draw a flying animal — perhaps a butterfly, bat or bird – on some stiff paper. Colour it with paints or pens and decorate with a few natural materials such as feathers or leaves if you wish.

● Cut it out and attach it to a stick on a length of string or coloured ribbon. (See page 65.)

Wind flags

● Cut some brightly coloured or white cotton fabric (old sheets are perfect) into long triangular shapes. The longer and lighter the flags, the more you will see and feel the wind.

● To decorate white flags with natural prints, place a leaf or common flower on a flag on a wooden board. Cover the leaf or flower with a small piece of newspaper. Bash the paper with a mallet (keeping your fingers out of the way) and then remove the paper to reveal a print.

● Attach each flag to a stick with double-sided tape.

You will need to experiment, as some leaves and flowers make better prints than others.

69

wind music

Listen to the wind Try recording the wind's sounds on a mobile phone or iPod. Does the wind roar or rustle, hiss or howl? Perhaps you could play your recording back at night and let the wild wind music lull you to sleep while you lie snug in your bed.

Wind chimes Raid the kitchen for whisks, wooden spoons, skewers, pan lids and anything else you can find that might make a noise, or look for tin cans and lids in the recycling bin. Try banging them together to see what different sounds you can make, and then choose some to hang along a stick.

Hang your wind chime on a branch or outside a window to tinkle and clatter in the wind.

make a wind sock

These colourful plastic-bag wind socks can show you where the wind is coming from and how strong it is. They're also fun to take running with you in the wind.

● Cut the bottom and the top off a plastic bottle or an ice-cream container to make a cylinder about 15cm/6in long.

● Pierce a hole in each side of one end of the cylinder and thread a long piece of wool or string through the holes to make a handle.

● Cut a large plastic bag or bin liner into a long tube-like shape, or perhaps cut out a more interesting shape, such as a fish or a snake. Tape together any loose edges on the long sides, but leave a hole at each end so that the wind can blow all the way through.

● Using staples or tape, attach one open end of the tube around the prepared plastic cylinder.

Stick on bits of colourful plastic bag and add long streamers to decorate. Let the wind fill up your wind sock and bring it to life.

44

make streamers for wind dancing

Long crêpe-paper streamers or ribbons are perfect for wild wind dancing, marching and running across a windswept hillside.

● Choose a special stick. Cut brightly coloured crêpe paper into long thin strips, the longer the better.

● Staple the streamers together at one end and then attach them to the stick with double-sided tape or some other strong tape.

● Go out in the wind and dance with your streamers, twisting and whirling them around you. The challenge is to try to avoid getting them all tangled up! Try wearing bells on your ankles to add music to your wind dancing.

● Can you make figures of eight or write your name with your streamers? Or run along and see how wind blows the streamers into wonderful shapes. Take care not to hit other people when waving streamers around.

flying a kite

Perhaps the all-time favourite thing to do on a windy day; you can buy kites of all shapes, sizes and prices, but why not have some fun making your own? Be sure to fly them in a big open space where they can't get tangled up in trees or overhead wires or fly over a road.

Diamond kite – All you need is a plastic bag and some lightweight dry stems; dead nettle stems are perfect as they are strong and fibrous.

● Cut about 20cm/8in off the thicker end of a long nettle stem. Make a slit in the middle using a fingernail or a knife.

● Thread the remaining thinner length of nettle stem through the slit to make a cross; the top of the cross should be about 10cm/4in and the lower part about 20cm/8in.

● Use masking tape to stick the ends of the cross on to a piece of plastic bag, stretching the plastic tightly. Cut out the diamond shape. Make a tail with the rest of the plastic.

● Tie some thread round the centre of the cross. Use a large darning needle to pull the

thread through to the front of the kite and then pull it through to the back about 3cm/1.5in from the bottom of the cross. Tie the thread to the nettle, leaving a long loop of thread at the front of the kite. Tie a knot in the middle of the long loop to make a smaller loop; this is the bridle, where you attach the kite string.

● Hold the kite by the bridle; if it doesn't sit flat, add a little more masking tape to the lighter side so it is balanced. Now go and fly your kite!

Feather kite – Birds are masters of flight because of their perfectly engineered lightweight feathers. Collect some feathers and try fixing them together in a bird shape with thread and glue; can you make it fly like a bird? Or if a kite seems too tricky, have a competition to see how far the wind will blow your favourite feathers.

make a sailing boat

Make a little boat from natural materials or plastic from the recycling box, and then add a stick mast and a sail, all ready for a windy day. Make the sail from leaves, feathers or perhaps plastic bags or some fabric from an old sheet. Go out to a puddle or a stream and see how far the wind will carry your boat. Don't forget to tether it on a long piece of string or some fishing line so that it doesn't sail off in to the distance without you.

Safety tip Always have an adult with you when playing near water.

wind wishes

Go out to the woods on a windy autumn day and see if you can catch a falling leaf in mid-air before it reaches the ground. You'll need to be quick, as leaves blow around surprisingly fast, but you get to make a wish for every leaf that you catch!

4

snowy days

48 white wonderland

Opening the curtains in the morning to see the world transformed into a white winter wonderland is such a magical moment. To really enjoy the magic, wrap up warm and rush outside to make the very first footprints and enjoy the special snowy silence. And why not become an arty photographer, and go on the hunt for unusual and beautiful natural snow sculptures?

snow angels

This is a fun activity when you are wrapped up really warm; you don't want the snow to find a way between all your layers of clothes!

● Lie down in some quite deep freshly fallen snow. Move your legs from side to side to make a skirt, and move your arms up and down to make wings.

● Carefully stand up to reveal an angel imprint in the snow. Can you move away without treading on it? How about making a whole row of angels holding hands or in a circle? Try decorating your angels, perhaps with grassy hair, pebble eyes and leafy noses and mouths.

50

make an igloo

How about enjoying your very own igloo after dark with lanterns and hot chocolate?

● Pack snow tightly into plastic storage boxes to make bricks. Tip them out of the boxes and place them in a circle.

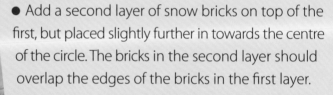

● Add a second layer of snow bricks on top of the first, but placed slightly further in towards the centre of the circle. The bricks in the second layer should overlap the edges of the bricks in the first layer.

● Continue adding more layers of snow bricks, each layer set further in than the layer below, until the walls meet at the top. Fill any gaps with loose snow and check each layer is stable before you build the next one. If the walls aren't going to meet at the top, you can always make a roof from wooden planks or a sheet of plywood.

● If a life-sized igloo sounds like too much of a challenge, try making miniature snow buildings instead. How about an igloo for your teddy bear, a white palace for a snow queen or a snow church for a fairy wedding?

51

make snow creatures

Why does everyone always build snowmen? Why not make snow monsters, birds or animals? Go out in the snow, find a few sticks and let your imagination run wild!

● Mould a snow shape and add sticks and other natural materials to transform the shape into an animal – perhaps a spider with long legs or a hedgehog with stick prickles.

● Push some sticks into the snow to make legs on which to build a creature such as this sheep with leafy ears or this chilly bird with snowy feathers and bright red berry eyes. Try making a whole snow scene of animals – perhaps a snow farm, a snow zoo or a collection of animals you might find in the local woods.

This reindeer was brought to life with lichen-encrusted antlers, sloe eyes and a Rudolph red nose stuck into his snowball head.

52

snowball sculptures

These snowy masterpieces will last only as long as the weather stays cold.

Hanging snowballs How about decorating a tree with snow baubles? Find a short twig and tie a length of string or cord on to it. Make a small snowball around the twig, and hang it on a branch. Decorate with thin twigs, feathers, seeds or berries. If the snowball is very solid, pierce holes in it with a pointed twig or a pencil. Use thin twigs to fix leaves on to the surface of the snowball.

Decorated snowballs Roll some big snowballs and decorate them with leaves, moss and other natural materials. What patterns can you make?

Coloured snowballs Fill some spray bottles with cold water and put a few drops of food colouring in each one. Make several snowballs, and put one in a deep bowl and spray with colour. Repeat to make more balls of different colours. Decorate a tree with your coloured snowballs or hide them and play hunt the snowball.

53

 snowy nights and lights

On a snowy night the natural world is eerily silent and luminous under its chilly blanket. Snowy darkness is bright and exciting: perfect for a night expedition, or perhaps some night sledging on a wide-open obstacle-free hillside. Or try a night picnic lit up by these magical snow lights.

Snowball lights Make a long line or a circle of snowballs. Push a plastic cup into the top of the first snowball, and then remove the cup and place a night light in the hollow. Repeat for each snowball, to make a magical trail or circle of lights. Alternatively, make a huge snowball, carve out holes and fill them with nightlights.

Dragons and monsters How about making a dragon or a monster out of snow, and then bringing it alive with eyes of fire?

Light holes Drop night lights on to the snow and light them. Once alight they will slowly sink down into the snow to create their own sheltered holes.

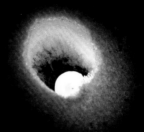

54

snow pictures and patterns

A patch of pristine white snow is like a blank canvas. What patterns can you make on it or what picture stories can you tell?

Collages Use natural materials such as leaves, seeds, berries, sticks and feathers to make patterns on the snow, or try making a collage of an animal.

Pictures Make a picture in a stick frame on the snow. This stick man has a coloured snowball (see page 89) for a head.

Storyboards Make a row of stick frames and fill them with a sequence of pictures to illustrate a story.

Snow stencils Use cardboard cut-outs to make stencils of coloured water sprayed on to the snow, like the Valentine's Day heart on page 81.

snow mazes

This activity is perfect for sticky snow. Start with a little ball of snow, and then roll it over and over until it grows into a giant snowball.

● Choose a wide open grassy area with a good covering of snow. Starting at one corner, roll a snowball along in front of you, rocking it gently from side to side so that it picks up as much snow as possible. You will leave a cleared grassy path behind you, and by walking directly behind the snowball you won't leave any footprints.

● Walk up and down and round about to make a wiggly path all around the open area: your very own maze. Can your friends find their way along the path to reach the giant snowball in the middle of the maze?

Alternatively, roll a big snowball and leave behind a giant picture on the grass.

snow slushies

For a yummy treat, have a go at making these delicious snow slushies, which you could even eat out of an ice cup (see page 123).

● Gently defrost some frozen berries, such as raspberries or blackberries.

● Go outside and collect a bowl of freshly fallen clean snow. Gently mix the fresh snow with the berries, a little caster sugar and some pouring cream.

● If you would prefer a slushy drink, replace the cream with fresh fruit juice.

Add some decoration – perhaps white chocolate stars or coloured hundreds and thousands. Enjoy your tasty snow slushy before it melts!

snow shadows

Bright snowy days when the sun is low in the sky are perfect for shadow hunting, with dark shadows in dramatic contrast to the bright white snow. Go hunting for your own giant snow shadow or have a competition to see who can make the biggest shadow!

● Can you make shadow sculptures, puppets or monsters with snow, sticks, feathers and leaves?

● Can you make shadow patterns, perhaps using feathers, leaves or sticks?

● Take photographs to capture as many different snow shadows as you can.

● Make a snow sundial; then go for a walk and when you get back see how the shadow has changed.

snow games

A white wintry landscape or park is the perfect place to invent snowy games. Here are a few ideas to get you started.

Snow golf Push some tin cans or plastic bowls into the snow to make a course. Stand beside the first one and see if you can throw a snowball from there into the second one. If successful, move on to the next one, and so on round the course. The first person to get all the way round the course is the winner.

Snow bowling Fill some clear plastic bottles full of water, adding a little food colouring to each one. Stand the bottles in a line. Throw snowballs at them from a prearranged distance. How many can you knock over?

Snowball rounders Mark four bases with mounds of snow. Split into two teams. The bowler throws snowballs at the batsman; if the bowler misses, the batsman runs round the bases while the fielders pelt him with snowballs. If the batsman gets round all four bases without being hit, he or she scores a rounder.

Snow coat racing Race with your mates over the snow on DIY coat sledges. Get into pairs. One person removes their coat and sits on it; their partner grabs the arms of the coat and pulls the passenger along. Best to play this when wearing your oldest coats!

Fox and Hounds tracking game One person (the fox) drags a twiggy branch along behind them, leaving a trail through the snow. Everyone else (the hounds) follows the trail. Can they find the fox?

tracking wildlife

Early in the morning after a fall of snow, you might discover something about the secret lives of wild animals and birds.

● Wild creatures leave clues such as footprints, remains of food, droppings (called scat) and even trails of wee. Try looking in the garden, at the park or in your favourite bit of countryside, but make sure you go out early so that you can find fresh animal tracks and signs before they get disturbed or the snow starts to melt. Take a camera, a notebook and a ruler to record what you find and then go home to find out more in a tracking guidebook or on the Internet.

● Try following the trails left by animals and birds. Where do they go? How many different animal or bird tracks can you find? Think about what creatures you might find living in the area.

Look at the shape of each track, how the tracks relate to each other and how big they are. Are they deep in the snow or was the animal light enough to move over the surface?

feeding the birds

When it's very cold and the world is blanketed in snow, birds struggle to find enough food to eat. Give them a helping hand by providing them with extra food and fresh water.

Food Mash up some melted lard with bird seed. Find a tree in your garden, at the park or at school – somewhere you can keep an eye on. Smear the bird food mixture on to a branch of your chosen tree or spread it over a stick and hang the stick from the tree. Alternatively, fill a plastic container such as a yoghurt pot with the lard and seed mixture and hang this up outside a window. Keep an eye on the bird food. What sorts of birds come to feed?

Water Provide a shallow container of water for the birds to drink from – perhaps an upturned dustbin lid or a frisbee. In very cold weather, if the container has snow or ice in it, make sure you replace it with fresh water every day.

5

icy days

icy scavenger hunt

If you look out of the window early in the morning and see a white icy world, wrap up in your warmest clothes and go out with your camera. How many different icy patterns and shapes can you find and photograph?

● Look out for hoar frost which smothers trees, leaves, hedgerows and grass blades in amazing layers of white needles and feathers. It only forms on freezing clear nights when the air is very still and ice crystals build up on any cold surface, as though fairies have sprinkled magic dust to make a glittering wonderland!

● Or try hunting for icicles. Where can you spot them? Who can find the biggest icicle? These icicles have formed around grasses at the edge of a lake.

62 ice tobogganing

Not enough snow for tobogganing? Don't worry: try ice tobogganing instead! After a really hard frost, go to a hillside and try hurtling down the hill on your toboggan. It will be a thrilling ride, but watch out for a hard landing.

Tip Only do this on publicly accessible slopes where you won't damage delicate grassland habitats.

63

ice games

Large frozen puddles or very shallow frozen floodwaters over a grassy field provide perfect natural ice rinks on which to try out some of these icy games.

Ice hockey Each person needs a sturdy stick, long enough to reach to about belly-button height. Find a chunk of ice to use as the puck and use the stick to hit the puck across the ice. How far can you hit it? Make two goals from sticks and have a go at target practice; or split into two teams and see how many goals you can score.

Curling Play your own version of curling by sliding chunks of ice, or better still smooth pebbles, across a natural ice rink. Whose pebble will slide the furthest?

Safety tip Never play on ice on or near rivers, ponds or lakes.

Ice skittles Slide pieces of ice across the rink to knock down a target, such as a stick, a carefully balanced heap of stones or an ice tower.

toffee ice sculptures

Try this yummy activity on an icy day, or perhaps after a fresh fall of snow.

● On a cold evening fill some large trays with water. Leave them outside to freeze overnight and make ice slabs.

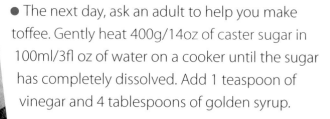

● The next day, ask an adult to help you make toffee. Gently heat 400g/14oz of caster sugar in 100ml/3fl oz of water on a cooker until the sugar has completely dissolved. Add 1 teaspoon of vinegar and 4 tablespoons of golden syrup.

● Bring the mixture to the boil. Simmer for at least 10 minutes until the toffee reaches the hard crack setting stage (when dripped into ice-cold water, it forms hard toffee and long threads).

● Ask an adult to pour some toffee into a small pouring pan or Pyrex jug (a small container with a spout will ensure you have better control when pouring the toffee).

● Carefully take the small pan or jug of toffee outside. Remove the ice slabs from the trays and lay them flat on the ground. Slowly pour

the toffee over the ice to make patterns or pictures. The mixture will set immediately, but you can add as many layers as you wish.

● To make a crazy edible mask, pour toffee in a mask shape and then push a lolly stick into it before it sets. You could make fine threads of toffee to look like crazy hair or whiskers. On a snowy day, make toffee lollies by pouring hot toffee on to deep, clean snow.

Safety tip Boiling toffee is extremely hot, so always get an adult to help.

ice lanterns

Imagine a magical trail of ice lanterns leading through the garden or the park on a frosty night. The more lanterns you make, the more dramatic the effect will be.

● Fill plastic tubs and buckets with water and leave them outside on a freezing cold night. The water should freeze around the sides and bottom of each tub, making a cup-like shape.

● In extremely cold weather the water might freeze solid, so place a smaller container full of pebbles inside a larger container of water. To decorate the lantern (see page 113), push leaves or winter flowers down between the two containers.

● The next day, remove the ice from the containers, using a little warm water to loosen it if you need to. Place one or more night lights inside each lantern.

For a larger ice lantern on a stand, place three sticks, each one about 1m/3ft in length, in a bucket of water. Once it has frozen, turn it out and you will have a large ice lantern on its own tripod.

balloon ice baubles

These beautiful ice baubles make great outdoor decorations in a cold snap.

● Curl one end of a length of fine wire into a small spiral and then feed the spiral end inside an uninflated balloon. The other end of wire should be sticking out of the neck of the balloon.

● Place the balloon over the spout of a tap and fill with water. For coloured baubles, add a couple of drops of food colouring to the water.

● Remove the balloon from the tap, and either clip a peg over the open end of the balloon or tie the end with thread.

Hang outside to freeze. Then carefully cut off the balloon to reveal an ice bauble hanging from the thin wire.

ice decorations

Hang these icy decorations outside a window or on a tree.

Pastry cutter decorations Arrange loose natural materials in pastry cutters on saucers placed outside. Place one end of a length of string in each pastry cutter. Pour water into each saucer, making sure the natural materials and the string are submerged. Leave to freeze overnight. Remove the icy shapes from the pastry cutters, using warm water to loosen them if need be.

Moulded decorations Soften a lump of clay or Plasticine by working it in your hands. Push a hard object such as a snail shell, an acorn or a plastic shape into the clay or Plasticine to make a mould. Pour water into the mould, then place some fine wire in the water. Leave outside to freeze, before removing the decoration. (See page 113.)

Ice block decorations Fill an old plastic container with water. Tie some string round a pebble or an empty snail shell and drop it into the water with some loose natural materials. Leave to freeze. Remove the ice block from the container and hang it up. (See page 112.)

ice windows

Hunt for ready-made ice windows on frozen puddles, or design your own windows and leave them outside to freeze.

Take some flat-bottomed dishes or metal trays outside and pour water into them to a depth of about 2.5cm/1in. Place a plastic beaker filled with pebbles in each container; this will make a hole in the ice.

Natural ice window Arrange natural materials such as coloured leaves, seeds or winter flowers in the water.

Stained-glass-effect ice window Add a few drops of food colouring to the water in the container. Once the water has frozen, loosen the ice by placing the dishes or trays in a bowl of warm water for a few seconds. Carefully tip out each ice window and thread string or ribbon through the holes. Hang up your windows outdoors and enjoy them until they melt.

Ice bunting Fill lots of small containers with different-coloured water and put a loop of string in each one. Once frozen, tie the ice blocks on a long string between two trees to make brightly coloured ice bunting.

69

ice pictures

● Smash some frozen puddles and use the bits of ice to make a mosaic-like picture on the ground.

● Alternatively, make pictures from pre-prepared ice blocks made in a selection of containers, e.g. plastic boxes, ice-cream tubs and metal baking trays. Fill with water and a few drops of food colouring (perhaps pink for a fairy or blue for a monster!). Leave the filled containers outside overnight to freeze, and then remove them and see what pictures you can make.

ice castles

Can you make a glistening fortress for an ice queen?

Natural ice castle Collect ice from broken puddles or the edge of a small stream. Choose a special place to build your castle – perhaps on a log, a tree stump or a rock, or in a corner of the garden. Fit the ice pieces together to make a castle. Spraying cold water on to the ice should help stick the pieces together. Add sticks and stones to make it stronger if you wish, and perhaps leaves covered in hoar frost to decorate.

Moulded ice castle Make some assorted ice blocks (see page 120) and use them to build a castle, a palace or even an ice monster's lair. Square blocks are good for walls and round blocks make great turrets. (For more ice castles, see page 112.)

71 ice sculptures

Collect ice from frozen puddles or make your own ice building blocks (see page 120), and have a go at making patterns, towers or even an ice arch.

Ice stack Pile bits of ice on top of each other, using the largest pieces at the bottom. The pieces should stick together better if you breathe on them or spray them with a little cold water.

Ice arch Build two ice stacks side by side, and try tilting them slowly towards each other to make an arch.

ice cups

How would you like to drink your morning juice from your very own ice cup or eat an ice cream or a snow slushy (see page 94) from an icy bowl? Leave a collection of round containers of water outside on a cold night and take a look the next day to see how many ice cups and bowls you have made.

tips for playing outside in wild weather

Have fun outdoors but please follow these guidelines, which will help you to stay safe and look after the natural world.

Leaving no trace
- All the activities in this book should be carried out with respect for the natural world.
- Respect all wildlife.
- Be considerate to other users of the countryside.
- Take all rubbish home with you.
- Take responsibility for your own actions.
- Only collect loose plant materials that are common and in abundance.
- Leave wild places as you find them.

General safety guidelines
- Always have a first aid kit handy, and someone who knows how to use it.
- Look at the weather forecast and wear the right clothes for the conditions. Use common sense and go home if the weather becomes too extreme.
- Avoid going near trees in thunderstorms or very strong winds.
- In temperate countries it is never safe to go on icy ponds or rivers. Only play on frozen shallow floodwaters over fields or large puddles well away from rivers, ponds and lakes.
- Always wash your hands after playing with mud, and make sure any cuts are fully covered with waterproof plasters.
- Be careful when touching extremely cold ice with bare fingers.
- Only use night lights and candles when an adult is around to help.

Fire safety guidelines

Always follow this basic safety guidance when using fire:

- Never make fire unless you have permission to do so and adults are around to supervise.
- Make fire on mineral soil, in a pit or (preferably) in a fire pan.
- Never light a fire in windy or excessively dry weather conditions.
- Never leave a fire unattended.
- Have a supply of water near by to extinguish the fire or soothe burns.
- Use as little wood as you can and let the fire burn down to ash. Once it is cold, remove all traces of your fire.

Tool safety guidelines

- Make sure everyone is aware of the potential dangers of using sharp tools. Accidents usually happen when people are messing around.
- Think about where your blade is likely to go if it slips. Before using a knife, make sure there is an imaginary no-entry zone all around you. To check, stand up with your arms spread out and turn around; you shouldn't be able to touch anyone or anything.
- Never cut over your lap – the femoral artery in the thigh carries large volumes of blood and if it is severed you will lose a pint of blood a minute.
- Work the blade away from your body, and away from the hand supporting the wood. Never cut towards your hand until you can use a knife with great control.
- Always cut on to a firm surface such as a steady log.
- If you need to pass a knife to someone else, always do so with the handle pointing towards the other person.
- Always put tools away when not in use; never leave them lying around.
- At the end of an activity collect all the tools.
- Knives should only be used when participating in craft activities. A knife is a tool and never a weapon.
- Give knives and other sharp tools the respect they deserve: always stick to the rules.

index

acknowledgments

Many thanks to the following for help and advice: Jane and Bob White; Roger Harrington (www.bisonbushcraft.co.uk); Rod Anderson-Boyle; Ben Haydon; Jenny Hanwell; James and Helen Jackson; Andy Rowett; Polly Scott and her reception class; Hereward Corbett and everyone who made boats at the 2010 Yellow Lighted Book Festival; Caroline, Colin, Clifford, Frankie and Anya Carr; and the many other families and friends who have supported us in so many ways.

A big thank you to all the young people who took part in activities: Anya, Clifford and Frankie C; Lily, Charlie and Toby R; Louie C; Carolyn S; Anna, Tim, Nicholas and Ella V; Johnny F; Freddy L; Rebecca and Edward W; Natasha and Adam H; Sophie T; Isabella G; Helena and Lucian S; David C; Milly H; Danny, Jess and Natalie K; Kate W; Tsering L; Kerry W; Libby and George W; Hamish, Isobel and Oliver M; Alexander and Mimi D; Josh G; Tristan L; Milissa D; Yanni K; Tallula, Noah and Poppy C; Hollie P; Ayrton and Edward K; Daisy and Monty S; Amy, Annabel and Matilda S; Megan S; Scott M; Daniel W; Rosie-May J; Tiggy and Woody W, Robi, Eduardo and Alberto MS; Christian L; Felix N; Jonathan A; Tom U; Joe B; Bradley R; Tristan S; Isla K.

Many thanks to our husbands, Ben and Peter, and our children, Jake, Dan, Connie, Hannah and Edward, for all their support.

And finally, thanks to everyone at Frances Lincoln.